You are my Greatest BLESSING

Written by

Saadia Isahac

Dedicated to my Ary Bear

Thank you for inspiring me and bringing so
much joy and love to my life.

From the moment you arrived, I adored you.

Your bright eyes and loving smile instantly captivated my heart.

With each passing day,
I feel an immense amount of joy as
my love for you grows.

You are getting bigger now and I can
see how much you are changing.

You are so much more independent,
and I admire your bravery.

I watch you and wonder where the
time has gone.

You make my days brighter with your hugs.

You ease my sorrows with your tender touch and caring attitude.

You make me proud with all your efforts and you teach me patience with your relentless attitude.

You give me hope in the midst of chaos.

You show me just how smart you are with your keen observations.

Above all, you show me what unconditional love really means.

Although being a parent is tough at times, I wouldn't change a thing because you make my life better just by being YOU.

You have filled me with so much
happiness that I only hope I can give
you back more.

You have made my world complete,
and you are more precious to me
than you realize.

You make me laugh every day and
that alone is enough.

I know how amazing you are, and I
only want the best for you.

I would go above and beyond to make

your life better because seeing you

happy is all that matters.

I can't wait to see all the remarkable things you will do in this world because your little light already shines so brightly, my dear one.

I am ever so thankful that you are mine, for you truly are the greatest BLESSING in my life.